No Matter

No Matter

POEMS

Jana Prikryl

TIM
DUGGAN
BOOKS

New York

Copyright © 2019 by Jana Prikryl

Published in the United States by Tim Duggan Books, an imprint of the Crown
Publishing Group, a division of Penguin Random House LLC, New York.
crownpublishing.com

TIM DUGGAN BOOKS and the Crown colophon are trademarks of Penguin Random
House LLC.

Selected material previously appeared in *The American Poetry Review, The Baffler, Brick,*
Critical Quarterly, Five Dials, Granta, Harper's, The New Republic, The Paris Review, Poetry,
Provincetown Arts, Raritan, Subtropics, The TLS, and *The Walrus.*

Library of Congress Cataloging-in-Publication Data
Names: Prikryl, Jana, author.
Title: No matter / Jana Prikryl.
Description: First edition. | New York : Tim Duggan Books, 2019.
Identifiers: LCCN 2018043688 | ISBN 9781984825117 (pbk.)
Classification: LCC PS3616.R538 A6 2019 | DDC 811/.6—dc23
LC record available at https://lccn.loc.gov/2018043688

ISBN 978-1-9848-2511-7
Ebook ISBN 978-1-9848-2512-4

Printed in the United States of America

Cover design by Elena Giavaldi
Cover photograph by Søren Solkær

10 9 8 7 6 5 4 3 2 1

First Edition

And when the parts disappeared their intelligent properties ceased being intelligent, and their unintelligent properties ceased being unintelligent.

—Daniil Kharms
(translated by Matvei Yankelevich)

CONTENTS

No Matter

Got

off a stop early but no harm.
A pleasant walk. This is a different place.
Lady at the counter doesn't know it either,
no use asking.
Lucky you turned when you did
and saw the ceiling of the Brooklyn Bridge
not ten feet above. Never noticed
the whole thing's umber, made of brownstone.
How same this town is, same as itself, unyielding.
It gives you time, almost, to make
observations such as this, it draws them out
like the East River pretending
to be a river when it's merely an appetite.
I'll take it from here, you think, I know the way.
Just barely convincing.
Then you saw St. Peter's down below, confirming
this is Dumbo
and thought yes, finally they've made it right
with Malta: set forth on the long downward path
of sandy steps a touch too long and shallow
for human locomotion faster than deep reluctance
southwest, Spanish gravel, attractive, toward the church,
when houses along the way start exploding.

Anonymous

Her hair is parted in the center and this side
wall of the house ends just above her part.
The seam between the house and not-house
seems to rise out of the part in her hair.
Dandelions on the lawn are playing
sundials, their globes give out the time
of year. She's not smiling so much
as grimacing against the pull of the brush
and squinting against the sun. Nowhere are
her feet more than tacit. She is the tallest one.

Waves

on the Hudson just a few inches
above the crown of my head, it's fall but the leaves
as green as the afternoons humid,
they fall from the trees a halfhearted yellow,
unswayed by the unforthcoming change.
How you crossed that island I don't know,
one of the blasts must have nudged you.
The Hudson is a river though, with genuine water
going one way most of the time, a true expression.
Not much else here, of the city I knew.
The doggerel place, a place you pray
to be delivered from through
not too much exertion of your own.
I designate the gondola
to Hog Island my second home,
may I get carried away in perpetuity.
Deliver me as down along a zip line—
these piles, these ornate cornices
best seen if not in enlargements of scenes
of Myrna Loy's xmas eve between
martinis then through the blinds
of function rooms where hopefuls in colorless
uniforms circulate edible miniatures—
even if the view going down differs
from the view going up.
The city welcomes you.
The cathedral perhaps, its smoking dome
still visible over the charred fastnesses
of Village and East Village,
still visible when I turn.
And here we reach the shores of speculation.

Real

In which the studio
grows L-shaped, with an alcove
for the bed, you modest dream, in which the railroad

widens sideways, new door
a sudden wing ought to invade the brownstone
next door, but that brownstone loses nothing in the dream

in which another room
it's huge, with grand piano and French doors
opening on a view of my private beach, why have I never bothered

going in this room before?
Those years obedient to time is money when
it's space that's time, every tenant diligently building out the common night

Waves

And the orderly whitecaps continue
pushing the weather to assert itself.
In hindsight the way those brownstones go off
in sequence seems quoted. If original

perception's what you want, go
—In no hurry? Why,
there's always a bodega with some bottles
of water left.

Bodega city, you tried thus
to pelt me with convenience in small ways
knowing the big conveniences would be withheld,
I think your effort was sincere.

I needed no Twix or bused-in muffins in
cellophane, but their availability everywhere
translated into a kind of human warmth.
Like human warmth, it was too much.

The pale skinny one had that aim
with punchlines that after an hour of shooting
things down I'm positive we—and later
waiting for a car a girl just as thin

and mean turned out to be his ex, I liked her
just as much, she could not hold it in
when I pointed him out, he'd be
married in three weeks. I laughed, happy

to just observe in this for most
second city, encamped between then
and then. Life would start another time,
meanwhile the capital always

another time, a constant prospect.
The girls I know look long and hard,
make lists, to-do, two columns
pros and cons.

Anonymous

The whitecaps blink like second thoughts
or action captured through a fledgling medium,
made sweet and anterior, already posthumous,
trinkets. A building of pale stone stretching out behind.
Stately, in other words.
Modillions between windows even at ground level and awnings pulled in.
Shadows short as a breath caught short,
midday.
To the right of these two, a third girl is centered in the center of the picture.
She seems to sway, making a window between her waist and that of the tallest girl.
We see through this window to a window behind.
But she leans toward the tall girl, cocks her head, and looks at you.
It's the look of a friend who knows you well.

Fit

It's the magnetic nearness to centers
of power that makes nearness a kind
of sameness and sends the needles haywire,
ordeal to just find a good tailor.

That Russian lady without
a huge amount of tact knew what to do
with a velvet dress the color of fire
bought on consignment and the handsome

Algerian near Tompkins Square
all hands-off deference carved
a linen dress three sizes too big to just
my shapes and knobs, and then I sent

my boyfriend there with a Hugo Boss
suit equally too big, and he hacked it
into something like a joke so that
was the end of that.

A shy person so razed
by the occasional leap beyond shyness that years
pass before she can smooth the bodice
of her dress down with both hands,

at last convinced being ridiculous
is not what they could accuse her of.
Shyness, not reserve—the reserved have less
to fear of what comes next,

the meadows, the shepherds
discoursing on the fitness
of the lobby of the Pierre for their
upland bivouacs—the reserved not only

sidestep facts but deal in forms
the shy find beneath them, scattered
about underfoot,
common.

Sibyl

I held a case

Sixth Avenue rewarded with a name for that undoing

walking up you turn left for west and right for east

that's all the map there'll be then

unfollow me

one of the most boring avenues

but then

but then all the avenues as a whole are more

because the streets are briefer, more self-possessed

remember?

I held a case

it was pre-war

I carried it onto the Avenue of the Americas

I went for coffee

this doesn't chronicle the time I went

in one of the dozen identical cafés on Sixth

so you can take my word for it

so you can take my word for it

I also am all about abjuring abstraction

I wasn't about to hand it off to anyone

not even you

listen

I'm no messenger

Friend

I said the wrong thing again but really meant it.
Her greatness threw me and maybe knew what I meant?
Benevolence of eminence I'm testing you.
You may not know when you are being tested.

You're on your own to make the miracles ensue.
Nowhere is protagonism so supported.
She's also alone but it's not her first event.
Are you more alone when you have experience?

Her mouth queues up the taste of that covetousness.
It leads to nothing else than what it started as.
It's criticism of books not art or music.

She's still the harshest judge of her own sentences.
She shelters in my character analysis.
She gets me in a side hug till I'm homesick.

Ambitious,

i.m. Ellen Willis (1941–2006)

yes, likely story
again takes me in, full ride
comically uninformed

though I got St. Mark's had long
performed itself, that little tea shop
named after a Stones song (a guy

explained it to me) I'd frequent
and pour my calories into making
rent but never really talk with Ellen

before she died—her silence, absolute
thrust my polite papering over my
silence into choking high altitude—

but when I went to work for Bob she said
distinctly there are things on earth
besides, what was her term

policy papers, that might not have been
her term—cut short, the city's gone
simulacrum

Little York, every great
city leaves a little city in its wake,
even Troy had it done to it

and the hero as he passed
through most complimentary,
his way of nodding to

solidarity, that's how he'd press
renewal out of those migrants of his
and something like this too

was her philosophy, but I am forced
to pour it out, her half of tea
would be to sit in silence, undaunted

words for paragraphs although I hear
she had friends too, friends she spoke to
well knowing it's no use telling

some things, they need situation
so much situation
the slant of land, tiny far-off crenellations

the need's so great they build a Little Troy
like I keep trying to tell you
I moved here because he meant to

it tumbles out, slope or no, as when
no telling what you'd be
without the one born before you

Greenpoint

A siren was widely ignored
as we slammed the front door locked
and went out for ice and votive candles.

The houses cold as lined foolscap
in a rainbow of pastels were with few
exceptions on fire, the siren a kind of derrick.

But you could hear it all the way to Vinegar Hill
downstream or up, depending on the tide,
and as we strolled to the general store

for soy milk and to preorder half
a dozen linkboys for the night, we hoarded
our luck. St. Peter's over the hill

was showing sculptures made
entirely from subway cars. We charged
our phones at the base of a traffic light,

what every semaphore was for. Almost time
for a weekly share from the nation's
remaining newspaper.

It not only beamed to the backs of our eyes
but was beamed there by us, optic nerves
the sites where all the news occurred.

Stoic

Upper East Side's where you want to cultivate friends,
its mediocre restaurants won't close
or send the delivery guys home on their bikes
with the hand muffs giant papier-mâché
ear horns no use against hurricanes;
you hear them coming but can't endure them.
In this city friendship's
the main mode of disaster prep.
Basements and subbasements busy
with boilers switching on and off
inflicting real wear-and-tear on just
the effort of getting in touch
with those you don't want to lose touch with yet.
I never saw the guys draw
their bikes through the subway's
emergency doors so they must steer
those ear horns deep into the outer boroughs
to sleep a few hours before pedaling back
to one of the ten or twelve downtowns
to do it over. Those the zips
real friends should have, and to be real
be necessary. Everyone has the one or two
friends from back then whose points
can afford to equal zero,
though not perhaps without some penalty
being inflicted all the time,
nobody needs more like you, so then
I found it in myself because I had to,
the one or two things that
make it endurable here, and what they
boil down to is indifference.

Waves

True little waves, from high above in a window seat
so few of you have enough of yourselves
to fold over onto, forming a dress

you wear out instantly, the most part
of you is continuous skin with its own living
texture curving over the bottom, a bone, though often enough

on land it appears you're falling
all over yourselves to be tallest, each of you
prim threat of drowning should I contemplate

a swim, the window seat is just a way of taking in
the danger all at once, breathing the ultimatum in
and trying to breathe it back out at decent intervals.

Asylum,

like when I can't sleep I say to myself
the the the the
the

the
the—
each article drenched to the bone in the

belief it attends something solid,
fond belief, always being
cut in on—the

the
the
the the the the the the

does the trick if I can stick with it
not get swept into narrative, that shock brigade
all tell, if by shock they mean hit

the the the the the the the the
papers say asylum is temporary
now, true, what's not that's able to

maintain its potency, you wake up
from a spell in that genre of safety, relative
safety, what saved you

making as if the story were widely shared
until you saw them as-if otherwise and then
what saved you was seeing their look, saying

resemblance too may be at any time revoked so
must be made the most
of,

seeing it then, seizing
the minute dismounting with the foot
trained as a dancer to keep you traveling because

they'd slept and, refreshed, moved the the the the
papers expired, it's their turn now
to really live

Anonymous

Above these three pairs of dark patent boots
on the highest of three steps, where three
of the six toes jut out past the nosing
making three little cups of shadow
hanging from the top of the riser,
each little cup falling over to the right
at exactly the same angle, three columns
of girls in long coats rise
between two dark pillars on a porch, three bright
numbers running down the right-hand pillar:
1
7
6.
All three wear hats,
each hat forms a porch
around each face, each face
smiles from its porches into the aperture.

Vertical

A stop late, sure, but who gets off the train
a stop early. You did, your mind
did it, as if to clear space
for some new arrangement. Miss it
and the knot leashing you to a place
tightens; disembarking one stop shy
raises the question of whether you plan to proceed.
As the man said, Whither do you follow
your eyes so fast?
Just walk and let the city's map draw you
elsewhere, somewhere else
with it. Rarely did I enter thus
into collaboration, so cold
it seemed to surprise myself.
I consider it a measure of the distance—
far be it from me—the idea of going away
had gone. Name me a city
as bullying as this one. Low, mean,
drizzling Dublin kept a grip
on her boys but let them go, all but
heaved them out. I'm allowed
to feminize Dublin because I lived there
too, she's a friend, a friend I avoid.
Mean as in low and dun,
the finest avenues the emptiest
and dingiest, endless wet radials sending
out one long Georgian pile, never thinking
to plant a tree or incorporate a café,
carpeted in the candy wrappers
of English chocolate bars blown among chestnuts
when a sudden gust brings back
the sun for ten minutes
morning and evening.
It too now shoots up panes in air
clenched in the teeth of cranes
rearing at the mouth of the river,
that rinky-dink river. You have to live

somewhere, yes? The information
of the city, any city, will submit
to redaction for, yes, him
financing the air up there,
the shadow real estate. He throws
up home on home on
around the park, which grows
a shade garden. The other way
has always been so wide and long one part of it
will wait three days to hear
it's been attacked and in effect
is gone. Forming an ensemble
cities sing together in chains
of hand-holders around the globe
during the cold war, releasing their little
fictions with consequences.
Singing you're free to try them on, the bigger
the body clock the stronger its pull
and cities' clocks eclipse the planet's.
That's how they get you
that building frenzy, each one avid
incorporating another's thought
into her own in order to become
more herself until the place
is solid masonry.
Cafés on all the streets, yes,
it's one and the same café, you're welcome
to step in it twice. Stay too long to afford to move,
you're free though to jump off the B
before going too far
which is far enough.
You have to steal away, in the night
while sleeping.

Snapshot

When the floods came, washing out tailors
with small square change booths whose fabric
portals never entirely seal you in in dry cleaners
it helped to have done this exercise.

The luxury of each ending's weakness
for order is the time afforded
between falls to picture what will follow.

No one seems to mind
the season at Fort Tilden stretching
to October, even right-thinking people celebrate
by turning the phone on themselves, the sea behind.

For accuracy in prophecy perhaps
it helps to be unmoved by beaches.
The digital files speak and decompose.

Sibyl

The officers wear plain clothes for weeks
then unannounced for months will dress in uniform.

I assume this is intended to keep me in
suspense as to the nature of
the structure of authority among them,
two of them keeping their distance
and one walking beside me,
a little behind, always talking
into his walkie-talkie
to the two.
It was the one not the two that time
joining me in the sauna
with his walkie-talkie
sweating but still able to function.

I kept my swimsuit on.
I felt the molecules coming and going.
The atmosphere of the sky is also called an envelope.
Why they bother steaming it open
to black out certain clauses
is beyond me. No, they want to keep me in
suspense as to their interference up to and
including the moment I slice it open. Suspense:
I've learned to let it hold me like a refuge.
My margins have it in them
to move backward and forward.

Friend

Montaigne was right, without the body's meddling love
is more thrilling.
Yet from the start in elementary what she did
with it was far
from irrelevant, her jeans, mascara, rings all
articulate.

And she was always so pretty. Claire Birchall of
the yellow hair,
the twins at my birthday party came out and told me
I was unfair
for only playing with her. I said I was sorry.
I didn't care.

Bev across the street who shielded me from Bridget,
nightmare next door,
not nothing. Then Bev in high school who spared me
the group disease,
four or five girls forever demanding IDs for safe conduct.
I broke up with

her over God (she believed) one lunch hour and after
that was alone.
Then Jenn in freshman year, devoted and dumped me
when I moved in
with Jess in sophomore, who was it. That went on and on
like family.

Then Mary, then Mitzi, then Steffani? How the names
now overlap
as if slackening, hardening, deaccessioning held out this
form of gushing.
Self-flattery. The rush of love's akin but it's only the
one I adore.

Insta

And do you suppose if there'd been phones that
Dido would have chilled, monitored his posts
as he sailed into a storm, the photos
parading purple cumulonimbus

and a zone of tender green oxygen
above the horizon, all backlit deluxe
with abundant cash and unspent prestige
of masculinity when he demurred

and beelined back to Sicily for yet
another game, and settling in to hate
read his captions and text them to Anna

she'd not forgive him, obviously, but
regroup, restock her selfies, renovate
her city for posting in panorama

Bowie

David Bowie drove.
Five or six piled in a
van but I'm seated right
behind him, whose driving's
not bad, it's good but
fast, faster
and so I clutch his hand.
Idea's to show us
the city.
It is an elsewhere.
Brushed steel Dolomites miles
in the air
with highways scored on them.
He made me get out
once and swing
those miles up
in a sort of bucket
to touch, swing
over and feel with my
finger the side of a
mountain, quilt
made of steel, each knotted
thread briar of wire.
With my fear
of heights I made with that
live current a circuit
to please him, and made it.
And the whole
long day he
drove he held my hand up
over his shoulder
tight in his
hand, gripping,
no danger
he'd let go,
antidote,
so though he seemed never

to hear me imploring
Please slow down, I could not
love him more.
And when he dropped us
off beside
his ocean, he driving
on in, us
planted there at a loss,
I texted everyone
y slash n
canvassing if given
the day's events I might
text him, be
expected
to text him
to thank him, my sneakers
sinking in
sand, blinking,
clutching my phone, holding
out for a
y

Salon

We spread our hands out just like friends
their posture is a kind of crouch
you wouldn't call it kneeling
no, look, they bring their

elaborate efficient arts to bear,
and instruments
of war, a redesign
for commerce here and aimed

at us they find their mark, the end
of every digit or
we'd hold the tip, or would we, it's

the one place no one has to talk
and nobody feels guilty for
their place, thank god for all these little knives

Fulcrum

1.

Across the river her voice sends shreds
torn from something gelid, all acute
angles though the surface of each call
is fur and dust. That last body a wraith
of small bones leaning forward whether
to blow her curses out or suck her souls
back in, it's hard to say. In practice today
the coxswain's miked. Degraded sound,
a scene with unidentified
afterlives shrieking on background.
I saw the bursts
of drives pulling her between recoveries,
her profile pausing against the far bank
as it raced along, hard to see.

2.

This city with its circulatory
root allows you to turn the time halfway
around to face the other way, and so look
back as though you were the one
you were eating with at that hour
your mouth full of her thoughts
when refugees are weaned in camps
and feeling as never before
with the distinctness of tiny folds
at the edges of documents seen
cascading back into the distance
where one of them must be
the first to vanish
what was wanted of you

Stoic

I like ordinary days. Needing to be somewhere new
at ten a.m. bothers me. I like ordinary days.
Each juncture where I could miss a connection is trouble.
I like ordinary days. Out-of-the-ordinary
days I live through many times. I like ordinary days.
You only live once and if that's true for you then you win.
I like ordinary days. Doing the usual thing I
can forget it's happening. I like ordinary days.
Living once is excellent and living less is better.
I like ordinary days. I like never having plans
and not seeing any friends. I like ordinary days.
I like my friends a lot when I'm free to think about them.
I like ordinary days. I like running into friends
in the course of my routine. I like ordinary days.
My friends should accompany me on ordinary days.
I like ordinary days. To be so accompanied
would be nice once in a while. I like ordinary days.
When friends come by with no real plans I want to get away.
I like ordinary days. I want to be alone so
I can think about my friends. I like ordinary days.
On ordinary days I don't need to think about things.

Bender

Cruising once in the North Sea
a mail boat sights a defection
off, let us say, the port side.

How long he froze there a mystery.
Medics couldn't help him.
He wailed Eastern European noise

they held him down. Bilinguals made
no sense of it. Till a chemist
with Cyrillic passing by the sick bay

unfurled it: C_2H_6O.
Following swigs of elixir, sailor
lived. This found me in a pub in Dublin,

my lady of the delay tactic, where
when it wasn't raining a very fine mist
gathered under umbrellas.

Coat flung over my knees in that
one-window bedsit I turned
the pages of *Moby-Dick*, starving

for what flared between Queequeg
and, let us say, Ishmael. They'd done it,
stirred, swaying

wits as well as the mordantly
dry Dubliners, out
of history. Free to dabble in the arts

I'd come to learn about, the
international arts. An Irish decade
and the West all over, was it, makers

manicuring lawns untroubled
for once. Bygones
watering begonias.

I'm just in time to see what beauty is
when it's at home—oh! shipmates!
on the starboard hand of every woe

there is a sure delight, and higher
the top of that delight, than the bottom
of the woe is deep. For heavy

traffic in that waterway, empathy
is out of order, take the stairs
marked sincere interest, nothing fancy

just an appetite. But then look around
a little. But then bestowing interest
on what interests you,

this is a crime? But then
voracious was a look I loved: Is not
the main-truck higher than the kelson low?

Now in the drink it's the sermon sticks,
distilled of the wish and then again the wish
it were so. So I swallowed it.

Anonymous

Just in front of the porch steps, on a flat stone
that appears partially tucked under the porch,
a ficus in a clay planter. It produces
strange sounds. The silence that comes dressed
in not the past but conditional tense
may be quietest, it's endured the most.

Shades

The island trumpets these
feelingly elongated gravestones.

Slabs perforated with windows and workers—
hollow, available,

you can enter any building now—and lunchtime
hypothesized our bodies being one,

partaking of a single bolt
of material much the way the clockwork

symptoms of a virus argue
against your uniqueness, though you groaned

uniquely, did you. Even so
the nature of your relation to chance

was a thing you couldn't know
unless things were really very

irreversible. And though you couldn't
you named it, dressed it up or down

oppressed by the depth of your knowledge,
archaeologist

of your own actuarials
in exile. Hearth fires burned in the squares

of windows closed to you all afternoon
till the sun went down into Jersey.

How entitled not to feel nettled
you felt, how lonely, how cozy.

Waves

winking their froth, their whole
body an eye, unhearing, unsmelling,
whitecaps far north as Hell's Kitchen

At first so far from framing itself
in waves it put a ceiling on itself
at first, but every wall becomes a street

Let it take so many generations, it will seem
a street had been intended all along,
whitecaps winking right and left

Waves the unstable ones, burn up
and fall down, consuming
themselves, theirs the permanence

Candidate

There I was
again in the anteroom waiting for news and saw
he's not white which did
make me wonder but I wasn't good enough in every other way
and wasn't going to tell him
how I felt, which was strongly
and the admission process was hard,
Columbia business degree, after a moment
of reflection I knew the angle my essay would get me in
but not how to deserve him, no
that's never going to happen
and accepting it's a solace
in proportion to how much closer it moved me to myself,
almost overlapping
as he shot some kind of javelin into outer space
(nobody else could)
and hit a god (pin the tail on), who got him back in a mortal way
he'd always be needing remedies for

By now he was played by a white actor I'd always found unwatchable
but I liked his resolve, the stoic way
he went every week to buy over-the-counter remedies for his injury
and even said it improved him
to own his own extinction,
it was not at all strange that dying conferred whiteness on him
as they sought a new principal
for the charter school, again
I'm unqualified but my commute is less than expected,
much of it through a park
in midtown, landscaped with gravel walks
and a gradual ascent like an apron all the way to our storefront
apartment with the verdigris bathroom
where an end table forms the vanity,
our child is safe here with us
though they approached me on the train while I pined for him
in an unsuitable place
overlooking an underground atrium.

Murder

To spy on them my calling at three
or four (a cousin down the hall
the informer), small enough to be one
with the back of the sofa, armchair,

the night we all saw (they unaware)
the gray face of a woman
like máma flash on the evening
news forever, its passport size

exploded through the living room,
when was it I gathered that dissolve
was native to them, how long after

I gave myself away in the corner
did the tranquil way they defaced her
come back to me

2016

Trusting no one we brought our first and only
to the party, who'd blame us for having
a flattering evening clocking
the imprints of our friends.

Thoughtfulness drew with a huge
compass a circle on the hardwood
so the hole for falling through
would be clean.

Second city of one mind,
the flash which alone
shows everything
so much so that after you close your eyes

the valley lives
whereas those slow good
questions, the visitor leaves going
they know very well what's coming.

Even things you
set in motion may grab you
from behind in a passage as though you
were part of some larger scheme.

At that time I'd already dreamed
of doing the impossible—
I was a woman at that time—
but the place was a heritage forest.

My hospital gown was elegant,
airy and boxy around my thighs
like a press release and the women in the ward
weren't saying what they knew.

My bed was the invitation
to balance on a log
near a stalker's altar and let nothing
of my thighs be exposed.

The damp was material,
greens and browns 3-D as pleats
on mitochondria, each particular
could swallow you.

It's not that the forest takes your baby
just you might want to avoid
having a baby in the middle of the forest.
The whole world's full of newborns now

more so than usual, yes,
and mothers saying are you kidding me
including those without children.
Who joins me in asking pardon of this boy

for the year that fetched him in?
Not so fast. If the fault was always here
but hidden, isn't it best
to have it out?

A figure for this that's just
does not exist and a hero would cut
a figure so I continue pacing.
Heroism's safety, I thought and thought.

He is soft, he glows
when I smile, he plants his whole face
in my neck, the locks
of abstraction on visible things collect around him.

From a distance as though it were walking here
the thought grew taller till I saw it
as I held him one morning,
what'll he do with a bit of strength.

Mud and dust and stuff I can't describe
push his feeling deeper as he grows.
My memories all feel like news
as if I've been good at getting them wrong.

Sibyl

I have a case

If you know the code
you can try it up to three times
thrice her shadow fades in my embrace
and then it's locked, good luck

I think there's an Apple on Sixth
you can map it on my phone
if you have a way to verify your picture ID
is yours, you're fine

They accept three forms of resemblance,
one) bottle of imported wine
two) pair of authentic Levi's (right size)
three) exit visa

If they also accept resemblance
as a phenomenon, you'll not
be interned with anyone
who doesn't speak your language

Prepper

Fine, cruise ships fail to dock
on the Upper West Side, a special sort of hell
takes shape on eighteen decks
when supplies run out, decks
so high off the rock
of the waves the impact
gets them before they get
the chance to drown
and the climbing wall, still there, receptive,
testy as it says it is, gathers dust.
There follow debates over whether
we can drink and who has the right to
the run-off from the genuine skating rink. . .
To make it paradise you'd wanted
ocean there, everywhere, just
put down, put in its place
with a giddy violence
that then redounds on you
when things go south and that too
you imagine you embrace. . . Some things,
the philosopher said,
are up to us and others are not.
Since he said so
how the spectrum has stretched, or grown dense
with things.
Up to us are

Now sit and map the probabilities, fire
or ice, you won't be required to choose.
You want to learn to play both sides
to prove the self, prove that although it partakes
of existence it also exists. Should the western edge
of the Atlantic hold the eastern edge, where France
meets Hungary, may yet do a little dance
of erosion to prove you
among the vineyards and the vicious
impenitent weasels. They like creatures

of the deep within their rows of waves
slithering and silver have every right
to be seen and feared before the waves
crash over them. . . Fear, you see,
is a kind of love.
It's all you need.
It's nothing like this creeper gumming up
the wheels of the Corolla on our private drive,
what the day lights as well as the high beams
make of all roads and all forks in the roads.
Appian Way, autobahn—those folks'
wildest dreams too were escape routes.
But to man the *Symphony of the Seas*
her eighteen decks alone
with maybe a girl in evening dress waking onboard
that takes vision

Waves

The wind reeled up Broadway kicking a plastic bag
as high as the window cleaners at 57th Street, bringing hands
to lapels as hairdos slapped sideways and up.

Sunlight hit the wind,
wind fell through the light,
and everybody all of a sudden fought to hold a disassembling trapeze.

That night the wind remade itself
and shot down Third Avenue, now a black wind, clearheaded,
soaked with dark water repeatedly and repeatedly wrung out.

To walk up the street was to be rinsed,
to lean into the current and hear
its drowned voices, hear the one voice just stating the obvious.

Bräunerhof

This is a different place,
I had to change it slightly every day
so as to send it out. And then having

saved a few years
I move me
to the places they lived, a pilgrim,

and get no closer yet the hit
(as good as knowing her to think that dad
two or three languages away

was one
when she entered the river, he formed
against the bombs that left her London

houses undone)
is genuine
if temporary.

Even the saying so takes too long
and you turn earlier, arriving
at a neighborhood without the storied cafés

and their patina of dead patrons
whose books outgrow your capacity to love them
or one or two of whose books.

In this neighborhood the cafés unborn
or been and gone (exhilaration at losing
possessions, she wrote, is odd—

the relief—why, you're freed or
they can't be lost again?)
leaving sidewalks and solid structures

like buildings, like ruins
that shelter their motives
and won't say a word to you.

They only loom.
We lost our minds when the crisis came
(the loss a kind of unveiling)

and now to piece together how they'd see it
knits sweaters too small, but we knit them
faithfully distractedly

on the subway and/or watching my shows
knowing they won't really fit.
When I see you knitting on the B

or drinking in
the hair and interiors
lighting your phone

I give up. I guess
those habits of industry can't hurt
and what doesn't hurt you is useless.

Is that not the most gruesome impervious ooze
of the story? that it
it needs to be renewed.

Manhattan

Near the top of the oval portrait
the outline's ink enlarged
on a piece of privacy,
dropping down to water providing

for unintended trees, the crest
of money's indifference, undergrowth
at the edge of the city, stray leaves.
The Circle Line plies an O

round the island and roughly a dozen
people agreed to freeze, hunkering
mid-Feb in its low dingy arcade
for my birthday. We rumbled past

this nowhere at large, behind
the backs of the knees
of pale concrete foundations
years ago when I was young.

Jeté

It's easy to forget
that jetty that viewing
deck where we took boys and
girls on Sunday after
noons to see the planes goes
forward not back in time,

all the time unearthing
one picture after an
other of the woman
and her smiles, her magnet
ism (though had it made
him her object how slight

its motive force would seem)
all the time it travels
time peeling images
it flies on to deter
mine will or won't, that's why
it needs seeing over

and incessantly for
ward laying pictures down
around the obstacle
of war, imagined
war, but every war's first
of all imagined, made

imaginable, how
else make peace with losing
them, our own darting a
round this Sunday, to pause
in picturing it would
be unbearable

On

a beach you could reach
by water taxi they threw
this party, beach maybe
forty feet wide—

trucked in to show
in a *granular* way
how fine for folks
like us to settle down

by—and forty deep,
big plastic palm
trees propped like
cocktail umbrellas,

Pet Sounds booming
inside a chain
link fence, this or
that birthday, boy

I'd stopped seeing
for the boy in
L.A. brought a girl,
she shoulders this

tote bag I've got,
no beach for me
on planet earth,
open-and-shut.

Santo Stefano Rotondo

Come, walk this path
between flapping tarps
holding back on either side
construction sites

the way a bedsheet hides
from her her labor when
the scalpel's in it, come along
behind one friend in front of another.

Looking back the path narrows
(memory a scarce resource)
and bends, takes on the gentle
curve of the earth as if in the space

of that city it were given your body
to feel for itself the four inches
up and four inches down
per mile the planet swells.

Come and look at the frescoes:
they pucker with little logs
each round end is red
with a little gray circle in the center:

on each horizon (belted
from sea to sea) the dim awakening
potential for something equally made
from ignorance to rise up

all of a sudden is forecast
and if to get to safety slowly,
laboriously, circumstances draw
the flip-book of the city unbuttoning

one building at a time until it stands
revealed in grasses, slaves, with little jugs'
worth, little necks
of red paint splashed among

the pastures and meadows
and symbolic birds, and dewdrops
everywhere red, then who am I
to call it unconstructive.

Stoic

You know
how what pain is
for is brains, how be
capable without a line on

pain and how be here for any-
thing incapably, first you must admit
that pain has a body and if it can be cut then
can be sewn up, prepared to spare you admission

to its gut and not going there helps you stomach every-
thing, in the long run exposed to more of it, or how else play
fair in capture the flag, a touch of the surface there then rush back

to your side and interviewed hugging the trophy you'd not ask they hear
the question sealed inside your version—it was hard and my own momentum
toward undoing kept me from it—though you'd want to ask, you'd be dying to know

Friend

Gentle sincerity the color of fruit,
exes troop by, a beauty pageant

There's Kris in a Brazilian wax,
she topped my efforts collaging cards
and mixtapes (take so long to glue),
slightly on edge those two years in our
two-bedroom on the sports-bar side
of Gramercy, I think we both knew
I'd not be unlucky enough to
even the seesaw she couldn't unsee
and I'd still now deny was unbending
at its own dignified pace between us—

Is it the city that lights each debut
so professionally and choreographs
each entrance a celebrity, alone

There's Mel with a French manicure
(taking swipes) whose monologues
undid me, her fluency imparts this
almost physical feeling I'm reaching,
reaching to assist her in laying tarps
over the silence, any old hole we'd
come to and diverge around, if nothing
else I got so I could chart the New World
before journaling honestly told her
how to spare me that frantic feeling—

Or is friendship quite this
first class in every town and country
when supplies dwindle to zero

There's me with the microblading,
continual surprise tattooed
over my eyes at finding I'm again
an object of that gesture, an adept
since birth I'd say at reading the letter
of her meaning all the way in and
bearing it, allowing it a bower
in my musculature, see when I bend
I too suffer my build as an offense
and want, want, want it to be different—

Anonymous

One has the more organized face, a bowtie
producing a wide dark rectangle, like a strip
of censored text, at her collar.
The other's rounder, softer, and though both wear
half smiles of the same degree of satisfaction,
the other expresses contentment
more and thereby appears more resolute.
Oftener than family albums
I've taken down their faces, now
these faces float up with greater clarity
than faces I've known and that ease
of picturing confuses.
I must have known them well
but since misplaced
how they moved, which
more talkative, which I loved,
which preferred peaches and pears
just shy of ripe. Or is it that
their faces floating
always float up precisely in front
of what I happen to be thinking,
cover girls. No way their faces can be let
sit empty, must be always rented out.

Inwood

That quiet time before sirens
was a meadow of missed signals
except they weren't missed,
they were extraneous—noise.
Corlear need not have blown his trumpet
when he did, by Stuy Town
where my then friend lived.
Had he not that lowlands paradise
of polyglots survived official neglect
and rolled its carpet out into the vast
scrub of the country. With the onset
of sirens I harbored
these very specific longings for the hills
of Manhattan, they were so strong
I couldn't budge them into a line
of events like a package. So I'd think
what then, all overturned in subtle
ways, my then friend not enjoyed
parquet floors rent-stabilized with a girl
who ran a charity helping sick women
find gently worn couture clothes.
First they assemble out of scarves
a plausible figure of authority,
then they try to shine for it.
And studies show this to be crucial
for survival, all the more so
in the city. The appetite for that source
of light's implicit in the thickening
of undergrowth: this is why
undergrowth's so comfortable,
a relief, not a person
in the round, although my first time there
alone its stillness was enough
to breathe someone dangerous, a man
was tailing me. It's thick with freedom
from the transparent striving
of the trees, so I kept going

even feeling I'd be cut down.
That's how headlines are made
I thought and kept going knowing
this had been thought prior to many
headlines having been made.
We'd broken up and without planning it
I took the train to the northernmost stop,
walked to the last remaining hill
and walked its spiraling walks
up and down taking a new kind of careless
snapshot right and left, seeing
with sudden candor, which is
to unsee time. Distraught,
released into the nick between
before and after. The blank busy pictures
of nothing I took home then absorbed
a form of regret I carried on
past them, and grew heavy, so dense they sank
into one or another hard drive
it's years since I've seen them.
I tack up their memory
as if they were a reservoir
I might dip into again, though how
I'd bring it up without blanching
and blunting I don't know. It's as if
my muteness were integral
to the turbulence that brings new objects
crashing on shore. And one day
it struck me, what if I did nothing
to gloss the blankness, the chalk sound
of effects undone or words fished
from their glistening? So much rather
stay mum. That's how I gather
these keepsakes, a glacier strewing
drumlins behind her. The things
you're not yet equipped to say will not,
later, find their voice but reenact
themselves in costumes of their own
devising, portray their original forms
while facing backwards to study

the way it was. You'll be able to just
make out their backs and the backs
of their masquerades. And in that way
they shed the true development of time,
collate the then and then
into a stack of light, opaque glass brick
I like to think of as description,
dangerous brick. A sign that's what
happened in your country is widening
doubt that it happened at all:
failing to put it into words
circulating, inducing the news,
its tissue starts to decompose
in indeterminate ways,
which can't be done unless your mind
and every mind as it was then
does the same.

Lady

Wherever she goes the planes
of horizontals wave at her
their horizontal hands. The filth-

furry sills of restaurant windows, the increasingly
horizontal curves atop once
red hydrants, it goes without saying the passing

roofs of cabs and the little irregular ledges
on their handles, far from spick
and span call to her hands. They're confident

she's too discreet to use them as
the others do; her hands restore. And other men
and women when their shapes move

across not up or down, there
where they collect the motes that fill the air,
these surfaces she scans, no more than scans.

Is it out of habit or has habit been turned
and turned as on a spit
into an appetite?

Don't say the horizontals mean
anything to her.
They simply wait for her where others don't

like threats, but threats so ubiquitous
they're comfortable
waiting, like friends early to rendezvous.

Garden

Because of what I seemed reduced to
and I'd expected more
I wore this blank
effect
to the reception
not discouraged, willing
and only mildly tired though the lights
were out again east of Madison
and three or four helicopters hovering high above the little park

She'd have congress
with him on a bench they said
I pictured her backside
nodding at the bushes as he sat
comfortably, increasingly comfortably
and he would never settle, said that up front

Amazed they got away with it but then forgot
when bombs blossomed vast
orange anemones near the end
of *Clear and Present Danger* I came vastly thanks
to him, my fly down and others in the audience
saw what I know not, and that was in a small town

A Shake Shack now carpets the little park
I climbed to a railroad apartment
long in all directions, known as an open-plan office
the lights were out anyway
to signify canapés,
at large but shouting
endless prayer to shrink from every person who spoke
to me,
transaction

Waves

The whitemaned seahorses, champing,
the steeds of Manannan stolen
here, nipping

and eager airs. He closed his eyes.
He closed his eyes to hear his boots.
I am getting on nicely in the dark.

No harm comes to him on that curving sand,
then first he sees one of her sisterhood
lugged me squealing into

modality of the. Ladies,
whither do you follow your eyes so fast?
They are coming, waves.

Bob

i.m. Robert Silvers (1929–2017)

I think he found relief,
a kind of carnival, only in the tunnels

he forced, as with his body, in the replies
to questions he'd shipped by overnight.

This also explains why he swam laps.
Master of the deferential, intricate

refusal, lifetime ban on anyone
once deemed faulty, whetting his wrath

on the failure to secure
a seat on the aisle for that night.

And then he says yes,
yes, with a naughty smile

accepting the lesser thing
and raving about it

because when he accepts it
it's different.

Rubs out the sub's query
and rewrites it in his hand, his pencil.

Pencils sharpened a fistful
at a time by some sub-sub.

Walks in and quietly, melodically
says to himself

Any little news or calls or things
today or no one gives a fuck?

He bares his teeth, enunciates, and bugs his eyes
to be charming—You're all moving manuscripts

around my desk and I feel like Ingrid Bergman
in that film, what was it?

Gaslight!—and because he's a tyrant
I dry my eyes while laughing.

It's an uncomfortable fact (for
whom?) that those who went to certain schools

sooner found ways to resist him
or stop resisting.

The time it took me to see I'd never bring him
round to my view of metaphor's telling.

And then I proceeded
to pledge thirty more years to his archive.

Please understand
in tribute to him

I mean that literally.
When every man of letters was toppling

I thought this gives him
never dreaming of that kind of thing

yet another eccentricity.
Did he have material of his own, I wondered

early on, as if originality were invention, as if it weren't
some precision of knowledge and morality

applied to matters of substance, which among friends
we call taste.

Not that that excused my blinking
when he cut those talking in his vicinity:

he cut out small talk
not hearing it, convincingly deaf to its nothing,

although I suspected
he took in every word and filed it.

Romanticism too he consumed in its totality
knowing just what it was he demolished

as all the modernists did.
It being no accident his seeing what was coming

before going, did he regret his own
undoing any little thing?

Listen, he would start
when driven once again

to issue a rebuke,
listen, I'd stiffen,

listen—

Winter

This new habit of warm weather
sidewalks easing into catching up

prolonged in their confidence,
a traveled echo granted evenings

stretching into sports and
uniforms of practice

with dinners waiting just inside
open windows

whose checkered curtains
keep the secret of their color

when pattern/father and
matter/mother both were standing there

separate, solid
whose fault is it then, if not theirs

the fault keeps falling
between us, dispersing, how lucky

who doesn't love a winter
heat wave though its period aroma

its settled questions
smell so accurate the warm blast

carries something more, antiquity
of future time, the matter settled

Epic

Your friends of friends in the city
seduce each other in the strong light
of their ambition by reading long
chapters of long books to each other

not seeing, in bed with this poem
that two chapters want repetition
as though by the guy who made Rome:

You go Book I, II, III then II, III, IV
because the second night of his visit
Dido begged a redo and he did it

although if he glimpsed a new facet or
felt shattered to relive it, or bored—
her reaction tells us he said it
just as he'd said it the night before.

Heights

Hurrying down Court Street after work
to buy TP and a shower curtain
for C's weekend stay-over

I notice my *Hunger* protagonist
for the first time since January.
He looks less distinct (not quite as

near death though he's wearing
the same tight wire-rimmed glasses
and intelligence in the eyes)

probably because I identify him less
with the narrator, no longer being
so deep in it: "That strange city no one

escapes from until it has left its mark
on him," etc., though I'm just
as stuck in it. He asks for some change,

I give him my ones (three or four).
Asks how I am—"Okay
how are you?" Says, "You tell me,"

not bitter like how the hell do you think
but candid, as if he might like
my assessment. I guess he sensed

my reticence. We'd walked on and were
a ways apart when he calls, "Oh, miss!
This isn't a dress rehearsal, you know.

Enjoy it." Italicizing "Yes, thanks,"
by peering in his eyes, I hurry on
home to jot down my embarrassment.

Fox

Kitchen narrow
as a New York

kitchen, shape still
with me thanks to the

plate she threw, it nicked
his cheek, a mark

I tracked beyond
the crayon years

in Ostrava, never
forgetting *ostrá* means

sharp when the noun
is feminine,

and who will now
dig up why she

took up edges, smartest
in school, never topped

on lists surveyed
of boys of the

beautifulest, night
kitchen where she fought

his plan for getting out,
she lost, who loved

to love me most, they'd not
expect a little spy, they had one

time of day to have it out
though I would throw

a plate to make you talk
when baby naps, that's

prime time to write
these fragments out

and then he won
they freed us, bought

a house a Dodge a house
a Buick, I start driving

the Dodge they bought
a Civic, a forest

that was some time
ago, you and I

take trains to this
we rent, I get

to keep that night
kitchen thanks to that

one plate and her ongoing
appetite for seeing

people cut, her news
show is her need

to hurt someone
quite far away,

she's glued to it

Person

The reason it's modern to be fragmentary is the ancients had death and war
but a broken herm
was broken, omen of the approaching death in war and not a work of art.

We see the beautiful bizarre foursquare scarecrow with penis and balls growing
from the wall, penis almost
always broken, and miss the broken arms, crystal glittering in the discs.

I don't, though, miss them, maker keep your crystals to yourself, his balance
between person and
abstraction's so stirring I want no other token for anything can happen.

He's a person dragged away from personhood. The movement is ongoing.
A messenger insofar
as he lugs the unfolding news of his enduring. His message his undoing.

Friend

1.

Her voice cut through the talk before I turn
to see her coming in made pulse go cantering
and then our date to see the place—

then a basement restaurant with tropical fish
backlit in aquariums between tables
under brick arcades, more storm cellar
than ramparts of history—

where Julius Caesar expired
was nothing special, maybe we got
gelato after. But weeks after willing her
to ask, too big an ask in my experience.

So, scheming. To see anything
so long as it doesn't scream pretext.
In that sense how lucky we're in Rome.

2.

Not just the place but the cruise ship way
we're trapped with people speaking English,
it cultivates my cultivating favorites.
Group outings every other day, our routes
made little theme-park maps of the city.
Once a lintel to lintel pinned
our zigzags, each plane bent into a sharp
shallow recessivity by Borromini,

inhering so precisely in each
of his withdrawals. Started with the convent
at the foot of the hill, boutique hotel
that kept the naked brick façade he made,
small nipples tucked out either side
the entry, before the money fell through.

3.

Because I'd spent a Saturday alone
in Sant'Ivo (asked Bob before we came
his favorite place in Rome and following
a pause he named it) when we got to it
could drift so positioned myself
close to her. Wherever she was looking
inside that lozenge I saw it again,
surprised I'd missed the fracture in the dome.

Then onward to the single window
frame and less artless of two staircases
still jostling at the Barberini.

By now the power of all he declined
to do for clients, people like me
or around me who lose it over the
living and sighing flesh of Bernini
emanates out of each unpretending
stone I see admitting it's made, holding
its own against impartial admirers.

Sticking with them, dipping in and out
of puns with her. Never happier
than orbiting, free to store or shed
energy the nearer the middle of us
I step and put dumb questions to her
or taste my membership privileges
alone, bringing up the back of our set.

Anonymous

Their dated shoes are hidden in a cloud of grasses
of the kind she's holding in her hand.
The sound of a strand of wild grass ripping
has something human about it, you feel
the earth's scalp object, and that's where you assert
your difference from the earth, an unexpected
homonym, in your own perception
quickly forgotten of how a patch of soil
resists you and then ceases to resist
and then the grass is yours. This
great piece of turf, this photo-realism.
He looks into the device
with a face almost expressionless,
a subject very knowing. She smiles.
I'll be honest with you, it's difficult
to like the men in these photographs.
My contempt might be capable
of reanimating them, the men alone, so deep
does power lodge in them, no
that can't be right
when it's the soil
and they the famished little roots.

Sibyl

Tonight's host, the city

second city for those of us

we graze

there's talk of problems

distinguished by fine

distinctions, finer than you'd find

in other cities

aren't these the friends you came for

distinctions

and an amazing capacity for imagining

more than there really is

when that more helps William of Ockham show

Zeno nothing is a no-go

guests but containers

of capital

capacities

mingle

graze

nowhere on earth, honestly

is the turf nipped

to such a fine buzz

of knowingness

Snapshot

Because the needle at the top of the Chrysler Building
is visible now and then under whitecaps
slightly more of the Empire State
pokes up, like a buoy.

A coral garden Central Park
dreaming at the bottom.
Every shipwrecked cab and bus
noble in its sacrifice.

None but ethical barnacles tackle the struts of the Brooklyn Bridge
while hedonists lap the sweet water
still trapped in the pipes of Harlem walk-ups.

How pleased is the subway
to lose the distinction
of being alone in being under everything.

Coriolanus

Food, money,
contagion.

In a word
Bartleby.

But needs to say so
as is still

in business, has days
to fill not unlike Your voices!

ornately explaining
departure from this or that zone

of saying, whenever the net
diminishes (back-

formation into knife) into gouging
what had been felt intrinsic, this

truce, this just
let me live—an impulse familiar

enough, believe me. For your voices
I have fought;

battles thrice six I have seen and
heard of; for your voices

have done many things, some
less, some more.

The words say so
much less than seems

possible for words to say
they laugh at you, no each so

laughs at itself becomes
the consuming of itself,

a doing not a document, city
archive flaring, hand

on the volume
knob a dancer,

one spin turning it all
the way down, word

silencer, licensed
for burial. It's that

sudden. Tell me an act
more civil than this

disarming.

Vertical

One night the B took a turn
my ears popped

People in the orange loveseats facing forward
had to hang on

to something,
looking up I see

that man yawning at a pole
is uncle who never had a hard word

for us, who prospered
under every regime

He's young again and trying like everybody else
to find upright against the angle of the floor,

each car articulated
at a distinct angle, producing different pitches

of screams, no telling
how near the schism in the schist will bring us

to the core
Each person strobing past

on their own line
strains to hear the faint blurred station names

Stoic

At some point you have to walk to work
over those sheet metal cellar doors made
passable by those convex slash marks
marching diagonally through one another despite
very often that mutual hint, syncopation
underfoot, that they're not locked
and could open on the last abyss. Having seen
some videos I was dying to try a vertical
wind tunnel. Instead it's that tetchy
sweat wind hugging itself,
so inside you you spend it
on the faces in the car,
closer than a sleeping spouse
sending it back in your face
which isn't quite far enough away
for my taste from the now
infamous remark, We can have one
as long as it's understood that it's your
child. Who do I know who'd not depopulate
the city and be every man himself?
Give that man a raise.
It's once you reach a certain place,
in your thirties maybe, certain features
undo more of their significance.
Being able to twist and pull their names
from the sprue of an outer lexicon
is step number one. And step number two
may be endurance. Wait it out
I say, thinking the matter through.
Not easy, for you
are the one who's the matter.
That's when I hold off, don't send it,
question if I really want it, take a mini
vacation from worry, leave early
so I can feel that once in a while
I do get a minute to think.
And that's a step up, a bird's-eye view.

Optimism

Supposing longing prolongs the time
the jury's out

This city's long, you feel,
for a reason

You long to reel it in with a line
gripped in the hands or written or typed with the hands

reel it in from the future
back home

to its past, right now
And if the thing (arrangement)

they want is gone, they haul it in
around a beam

up from behind, past you into future and around
back here, having

first pounded in the fulcrum
with all their might, deep down, on some level

aware no fulcrum is that strong because
a fulcrum cannot long

Anonymous

The girl seen here second from right always levels with the camera like it's a friend.
But now I'm noticing the girl on the left, in the black skirt.
I like her temperature, sustained from one photo to another.
But I am supposed to talk about the others.
There are eleven.
Two prone in front and four kneeling either side of the older one,
each with her cheek resting on the next girl's shoulder.
They make a centipede of nine heads sloping gently
down from left to right, heads six and seven lowest,
then sloping gently back up to nine. Head five, the center head,
is supported by a dark narrow tie that hangs uncannily straight
like the letter I.

Sibyl

Hello

stranger

Who was it

got away if

you fled here

Bolted straight into the precinct,

congrats

Isn't there anywhere on earth

No, so

get off a stop

early

In a sense I beat myself there

nightmares saw them clearly

when I was four

Then walked right into it

here, Where do you think you're

Get off early, walk a little

on the sealed pavements

at an ordinary pace,

your commitment declared

It opens to let you deeper

into it, no knowledge

is safety

Dip

I thought of you then called you, each of us
reclining in our childhood basement then
I came over and your face was smaller

more crowded, not because of the two
pairs of glasses with transparent frames,
the bigger riding on top of the smaller

which I told myself was fine, and you were
taking off your clothes, even the tights
under your jeans which I told myself was fine,

they were sheer, so I tried on the old
feeling of being thrown in the shade
of your vast imagination—you were

knocking small objects out of your ear
with your phone and I did feel, was it
pity—then with you on top I gathered your

sweat in my hands and thought oh, I cannot
do this again, which would hurt you so
didn't stop you then your mom walked by

like she used to, without judgment,
she turned into the ocean and I thought
as I was waking up I'll take a dip

Binocular

Hanging there
here, everywhere, the doubles
the overhangs your looking past doubles unless

one eye's glass

the extras
we know to disregard, unsee
what the second eye adds until and unless we need

it the next

waits for you
but not relaxed, never less
than diligent in its shifting task, and asks nothing but

does depend

on that eye
containing more than glass
which renders it, as warmth, as memory, weightless,

unauthored

matter-of-
factly here leveling with you,
its recorded first-person vernacular selling it as

autofic-

biopic
to eyes one and two, it draws
them in to be together then they give it substance

a change of

circumstance
if anything's lost by this,
all of it, if it spoke, might name the cost of its wit-

nesslessness

inviting
you to look again toward
that country, never saying if it grants you time

to see it

Friend

Acquaintances not getting very far
until how was it in passing we found
we both at random times, crossing
an avenue with the light or paying

the humane sum with gratuity
for a handmade cup of coffee, become
convinced we're spying on an alternate
reality, our eyes surviving, while just

behind the moment prior we were
run over or shot, goners with tourist
visas undeserved and hardly know how

we got, but we got it, still got it,
seeing life go on without us
as we walk on calmly to the office.

Sibyl

I made another angry swipe at it
for I'd been told that anger didn't
put it off, disgust its antipasto, insult
a starch it loaded with various chutneys.

Was only following the script, to amp
that seer's eyeshadow, when it hit me
as riddles it scribbled on fallen leaves
were tossed up by the hottest breeze

that only a poet would make the tree
oak, those lobes, those tines would hardly fit
a syllable, and felt so close to one

who'd plant such little jokes—an orchard
ripening around the pits—while the seer sits
inside a stone and stuffs her face with it.

Waves

Explosions bigger than houses,
color of fire
in a period camera,

vandals
subversives
chain migrations,

in-
un-
date our expectations,

ACKNOWLEDGMENTS

The following poems were first published in these periodicals: *The American Poetry Review*: "Vertical," "Fox," and "Ambitious,"; *The Baffler*: "Fulcrum"; *Brick*: "Jeté"; *Critical Quarterly*: "Snapshot" and "Snapshot"; *Five Dials*: "Got" and "Fit"; *Granta*: "Bob," "Person," and "Santo Stefano Rotondo"; *Harper's*: "Garden"; *The New Republic*: "Real"; *The Paris Review*: "Friend" ("Montaigne was right, without the body's meddling love") and "2016"; *Poetry*: "Asylum,"; *Provincetown Arts*: "Friend" ("Her voice cut through the talk before I turn"); *Raritan*: "Prepper"; *Subtropics*: five of the "Anonymous" poems ("Her hair is parted in the center and this side," "The whitecaps blink like second thoughts," "Above these three pairs of dark patent boots," "Just in front of the porch steps, on a flat stone," and "Their dated shoes are hidden in a cloud of grasses"); *The TLS*: "Lady"; *The Walrus*: "Waves" ("The wind reeled up Broadway kicking a plastic bag").

This book could not have been written without a fellowship generously provided by the Radcliffe Institute for Advanced Study and a leave of absence granted by *The New York Review of Books*.

About the Author

JANA PRIKRYL is the author of *The After Party*, which was one of *The New York Times*'s Best Poetry Books of the Year. Her poems have appeared in *The New Yorker*, the *London Review of Books*, *The Paris Review*, and *The New York Review of Books*, where she is the poetry editor and a senior editor.